A is for anger that bubbles inside

You may start to feel it when somebody's died
It's like a volcano about to erupt
And comes out of nowhere, just trying to disrupt
But please don't ignore it, for know if you do
The anger won't leave and will only hurt you
So go ask for help, or perhaps scream and shout
Whatever it takes, just let it all out
And just like the ocean, it ebbs and it flows
The anger will come and then it will go
And slowly, but surely, as you truly grieve
the anger will lessen, then finally leave

B is for brave, yes I know that seems tough

with all of these feelings, you've just had enough
The weight of emotion, you're scared you might sink
But know being brave's not as hard as you think
For brave means courageous, and yes being strong
But it means letting go, you don't have to hold on
It's opening up and letting folks in
For with their support, every battle you'll win
So try it, dig deep, and summon your voice
Go look in the mirror, know you have a choice
To let the tears fall, to feel sad that they died
Be brave, little one, for support's by your side

C is for crying, those tears – let them fall

Imagine them bouncing away like a ball
Taking the sadness away for a while
And maybe replacing it all with a smile
Some days you may cry when you hear a song
Or maybe because you're not feeling strong
No matter the reason, don't question or doubt
It's better for tears to flow and come out
And slowly, so slowly, as you start to feel
Those tears that are flowing allow you to heal
For they have a purpose, yes really they do
So cry, my dear friend, they'll help you move through

D's for denial and just to be clear
Avoiding it all means it won't disappear
You have to have courage, face all of that pain
By traveling forward, there's so much to gain
And sure, there are some days you just want to hide
Bury the feelings, keep them all shoved inside
But I promise you one thing, if that's what you do
Those feelings get bigger, and scarier too
So please take a risk, share the things on your mind
Talk and release all the feelings you find
And know if you face the emotions with me
By fighting denial, you'll learn to feel free
brave
angry
Sadness
grief

E's for emotions, those things that you feel

That accompany pain and make it all real
There's anger and sadness, you will get upset
But smiling and laughter, that joy – don't forget!
Just trust as you feel them, even when it is fear
For Know there is always support somewhere near
Believe in the journey, there's no right or wrong
Yes really, those feelings, they all do belong
Emotions, they help you to face all the grief
They help you move forward, they lead you to peace
And slowly, the hard ones you've tried to evade
You'll learn to express them and find that they fade

F is for fun, yes you read that right

For even though grief may be holding you tight
You have to keep living, move forward, let go
Do all of those things that help you to grow
And know that the laughter, the giggles you hear
Do not mean the memories will all disappear
It simply reminds you, one day at a time
If you keep pushing through, every mountain you'll climb
So go now, do one thing that brings you some joy
Go call up a friend or play with your toys
And smile as you have fun, let out a big grin
And honor your loved one, for that is a win

G is for grateful, to always give thanks

But let me say something, yes let me be frank
For during this time when I know you feel sad
You'll also feel angry and even be mad
And yes that's ok, for none of that's wrong
But please do not stay there, at least not for long
You'll want to find freedom from all of the pain
And that's where the gratitude changes your brain
For smiling at something, for seeing the good
It leads you from darkness and out of the wood
Being grateful, it helps you remember what's true
That you truly loved them and they loved you too

His for hugs, you'll need them for sure

They'll help cheer you up, make you feel secure
Those arms will surround you, protect you with warmth
And carry you forward through all of the storms
And though it won't change things, those arms they will he
A comfort so special, it's better than gold
You're surely to feel it, the love that they bring
That slowly will fill you with comfort within
So when you are lonely, or you're feeling blue
Remember the thing that I think you should do
Go seek out a grown-up, a pet, or a friend
And ask for a hug, it may help you to mend

I is, "I", you're awesome, yes you; Go look in the mirror, believe that it's true

You're feeling the sadness, you're crying the tears
You're doing the work and facing your fears
And although you still miss them, the person who died
I know that they're watching - you fill them with pride
Their spirit still with you, the lessons they taught
Not ever forgotten, still held in your thoughts
And as you move forward, walk on through your day
Remember the words that they used to say
That you are so special, yes truly you are
So shout it out loud and say "I am a star"

I am ....
Funny
Courageous
Brave

J

J is for jealousy walking your way

That likes to stop by and likes to say hey
It usually happens when things seem just fine
And often sends shivers or chills down your spine
When you notice that someone has something you'd like
Or reminds you of someone who's gone from your life
The jealousy bubbles, it simmers, and grows
A green-eyed, big monster beginning to show
But know when you feel it, the jealousy rage
You don't have to listen, set it free from it's cage
Hit pause, then acknowledge, and then breathe in deep
Let jealousy go, it's not something to keep

K is for kindness, yes handle with care

You've just lost a loved one, it's really not fair
You're hurting, you're angry, the pain – it's all real
And just like an onion, those layers you've peeled
But now it's important you put yourself first
To nourish your body, and banish the hurt
Go soak in a warm bath, or curl up in bed
Do something that helps you get out of your head
Be gentle, be loving, call friends for a chat
And know you're deserving, no question of that
And what you'll discover, as you make a start
Being kind to yourself will help heal your heart

L is for laugher, yes go have some fun

Go jump in some puddles or play in the sun
For though you will them, there's on thing that's true
Your life's still for living, your time here's not through
So go on adventures, hang out with your friends
Tell silly jokes, or enjoy your weekends
For when you are happy you'll feel good inside
And it is important to have fun on this ride
And trust that they're smiling, the ones that are gone
Reminding you always that life does go on
That laughing is one way to fill up your heart
And help you feel close, like you're never apart

M is for memories, the things you enjoyed

From Birthdays to Christmas, or playing with toys
Vacations and travels, those trips to the zoo
The memories will always remain part of you
So take out those photos, the stories, re-tell
Cry as you share them, but laugh loud as well
For when you remember, the joy it can bring
That love that you treasured will sparkle within
And while there is sadness that sometimes can rise
And cause all those tears to fall from your eyes
It shows that they mattered, that you truly cared
Forever being grateful for all that you shared

N is for numb, for right now you don't feel

You're blocking emotions that help you to heal
You've pushed away friends, don't talk on the phone
You're hiding away and just staying alone
But please hear my message, that if you stay numb
The healing won't happen, you'll simply stay glum
That pain you're avoiding will always be there
That's right, it's not leaving, so please start to share
For talking and feeling, it's part of the grief
Yes really, by sharing, you'll find some relief
So please take the risk for I've truly no doubt
You'll start to feel better once you let it out

NumbVille

O is for okay, but let's be quite clear

You may not feel that way for days or for years
You're missing the person, their love, and their smile
You wish you could see them, just for a short while
But know as you wake up to start this new day
Remember it's okay to do things your way
For slowly and surely, the pain it will fade
So keep moving forward, do not be afraid
Your life will feel different, and that is okay
For now just remember, just get through this day
Yesterday's over, tomorrow's not here
So breathe and believe that you've got this, my dear

P is for pain, no it's not in your head

You probably feel it when laying in bed
You won't get to see it, the pain is within
It's part of the journey you find yourself in
For some it is headaches, for some a dull ache
That starts in your tummy as soon as you wake
There's no explanation for where it came from
It just seemed to appear when your loved one was gone
But know that it's real, in some ways a voice
That helps ease the pain you're avoiding by choice
And in time as you find tools, you'll cope in new ways
The pain will diminish, bit by bit, every day.

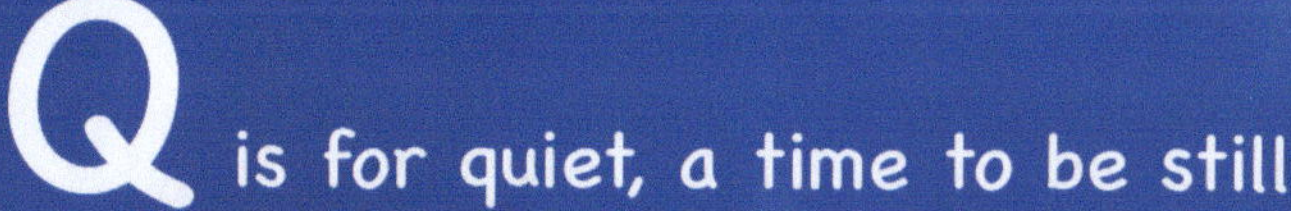

Q is for quiet, a time to be still

I know you don't like it, it makes you feel ill
But peace is important, it quiets the mind
You'll learn to enjoy it, just give it some time
For quiet allows you to breathe and to cope
To think of the memories, to help you find hope
To know that the anger, the pain, and the tears
Won't always be present, won't always be near
So please take a moment, yes all on your own
Reflect on your progress, the ways that you've grown
And know as you do, you'll start to believe
That quiet is awesome and helps you to grieve '

R is for reasons, the things you look for

Those moments you wonder why pain's at your door
Those unanswered questions that make you ask why
Why did this happen or why did they die
Yet here is the thing, those questions you speak
They're really not out there, the answers you seek
Instead what you do is you learn to let go
As reasons won't change the one thing that you know
You miss them and truly just wish they were here
To hold you and keep you all safe from your fear
But one thing to know, one reason that's true
The reason it hurts is because they loved you

S is for singing, sing loud and you'll see

The music and lyrics will help set you free
And while it reminds you of times that you shared
They're part of the process, to heal, and repair
So when you feel angry and you want to scream
And wish that what happened was simply a dream
Go turn on some music, go find a new song
I promise you one thing, it will not be long
Before you start smiling, as you sing the words
And give your emotions a way to be heard
For music's a language that speaks to your soul
And helps you release all the pain that you hold

T is for time, which sometimes goes fast
While others the minutes seem slow and just drag
You just can't remember the last time you spoke
And told them you loved them, or laughed at their jokes
For time is a thief that does not seem to care
Of how long it's been since your loved one was there
While others it feels like your time is on hold
You're stuck in a prison, your pain in control
But memories are memories, time cannot take those
No time can erase all the joy that you hold
Yes, time is a healer, that statement is true
but there is no limit for when to be through

U is for unique, which means only you

n know of the journey you're traveling through
d while there are others who've had someone die
eir journey is different, I'm not going to lie
t one thing's for certain, with them by your side
is pain that you're feeling can no longer hide
sadness, they get it, the grief and the pain
hough it is different, it's also the same
gether you'll travel, the journey you'll share
u'll start to feel better just knowing they care
d while your perspective is truly unique
gether, through talking, things won't seem so bleak
Calon y Mor

V's for vacation, just not in the sun

It means to hit pause on the work that's being done
To do something fun, call a friend, watch TV
Forget about things for an hour or three
For balance is vital, it's how you'll survive
To push through the pain and learn how to thrive
So pack up your suitcase, and please don't forget
There's no need to panic, there's no need to fret
Your troubles aren't leaving, you just need a break
To start to find joy as new memories you make
To feel like you're living, start feeling your best
Yes, vacations help you to feel refreshed

W's for weary, yes there'll come a time

Where you'll feel so tired, you're done with the climb
The mountain before you, it feeling so high
Your effort is gone and you don't want to try
But promise me one thing, please do not give up
The pain's not forever, there's life in your cup
So use all the tools and the things that you've learned
Then sadness will leave you and joy can return
For know if you're weary, it's just for one day
you've got this, keep going, it will be okay
Just rest if you need to, lay down on your bed
For feelings do pass and new hope lies ahead

X is for …. hmmmm, what word should I choose
For really there's nothing, no word I could use
It's simply a letter that's used in a way
To show something's wrong, it's not right you could say
But hey, wait a moment, here's what you could do
Take out a red crayon, or even a blue
And mark on a paper a big, giant x
One that's so big that you wouldn't need specs
And use it to let all the folks near you see
That you're feeling mad, or even angry
Or maybe you'll use it to tell everyone
That X marks the spot of how life can go on

Y is for yell, yes please scream and shout

It's really okay to let it all out
The feelings inside you, please go set them free
And know when you do, here's the thing you will see
That gradually now you will start to have room
To replace all the sadness, the blues, and the gloom
To cherish the memories, but start to make new
For that's what your loved one would want you to do
And when you are ready, some signs will appear
To let you remember your loved one is near
And maybe one day, when you yell what you'll find
Is that now it's for joy and happier times

Z is for zzzzz's, you need sleep my friend

And as we draw close to reaching the end
I hope you remember the things that you've read
And used them to help you move past all the dread
But always remember as you dream at night
Your mind it is moving from darkness to light
The pain, it has lessened, your life has moved on
And that it's okay to accept that they've gone
For no matter what, one thing that is true
They'd want you to live life, to keep moving through
So sleep and get rest so that every day
You'll honor their life as you go on your way